A

MW01118218

kind of

Prayer Journal

To Stephanie,
¡Prayer Warrior!
Blessings to you! ♡

(please doodle on this page)

This is a different kind of prayer journal . . .

This journal is designed not only to stimulate your mind when you're not sure what to pray, but also to make your prayer life personal, interesting, and even fun. Use the different pages in this book to guide your prayer and get you thinking. If a verse mentioned makes you want to know more, look it up and read the whole chapter – or the whole book. Use the blank pages for conventional journaling or whatever you like. Don't feel tied down, doodle in the margins, use colorful pens, and make this book about you and your conversations with God. I pray that this book is a blessing to you and helps you to grow in your relationship with God! ~ Samantha

> You could doodle here too!

Let's start with who YOU are . . .

My Name: _____

Date: _____

How I would describe my relationship with God:

_____

_____

_____

_____

_____

_____

Some important things going on in my life are:

_____

_____

_____

_____

_____

_____

How I hope to benefit from using this journal:

_____

_____

_____

_____

_____

My Best Friend: _____

Christian Mentor: _____

My Church: _____

Where I live: _____

My favorite place to be: _____

My favorite thing to do: _____

Other important things about me:

_____

_____

_____

Use this page to pray for a prayer partner, special friend, or anyone in need of prayer. Put the person's name in the middle circle with prayers on their behalf on the lines.

One of my favorite Bible verses:

Why it is special to me:

Let us consider how we may spur one another on toward love and good deeds. ~ Hebrews 10:24

What does this verse mean to you?

_____

_____

_____

_____

_____

_____

Trust in the Lord with all your heart and lean not on your own understanding. ~ Proverbs 3:5

What does this verse mean to you?

_____

_____

_____

_____

_____

_____

When I hear this song I feel close to God:

My feelings:

_____

_____

_____

_____

_____

_____

_____

_____

_____

_____

_____

_____

_____

_____

_____

_____

Cast all your anxiety on Him because He cares for you. ~ 1 Peter 5:7

What are you worried about? Ask God for help.

_____

_____

_____

_____

_____

_____

_____

_____

_____

_____

_____

_____

_____

_____

_____

Sermon Notes - has your pastor ever preached something that made you feel like he was speaking directly to you?

Write about it here:

_____

_____

_____

_____

_____

_____

_____

_____

_____

_____

_____

_____

_____

_____

_____

_____

_____

I feel closest to God when:

_____

_____

_____

_____

_____

_____

_____

_____

_____

_____

_____

_____

_____

_____

_____

_____

_____

_____

_____

_____

Draw a picture of your favorite Bible story.

I will praise you, O Lord, with all my heart; I will tell of all your wonders. ~ Psalm 9:1

I thank the Lord for:

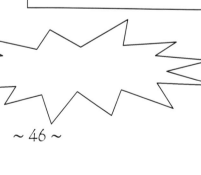

No one will be able to stand up against you all the days of your life. As I was with Moses, so I will be with you; I will never leave nor forsake you.
~ Joshua 1:5

Write about a time you are thankful that God was with you.

_____

_____

_____

_____

_____

_____

_____

_____

_____

_____

_____

_____

_____

_____

_____

Be kind and compassionate to one another, forgiving each other, just as in Christ God forgave you. ~ Ephesians 4:32

What does this verse mean to you?

_____

_____

_____

_____

_____

What does the Lord require of you? To act justly and to love mercy and to walk humbly with your God. ~ Micah 6:8

What does this verse mean to you?

_____

_____

_____

_____

_____

_____

Draw a picture of or write about what you think the ideal church looks like.

The place where I feel closest to God is:

My feelings:

Favorite Quotes

How I spend my day

This circle is 24 hours. How do you spend them?

Pray for God to guide you in making good decisions regarding where you spend your time.

The best book ever:

Why I love it:

_____

_____

_____

_____

_____

_____

_____

_____

_____

_____

_____

_____

Draw a picture of what you think Heaven might look like.

Where can I serve?

Part of being a Christian is serving others. From time to time it is a good idea to look at what you are doing and make sure it is where God is leading you.

Areas I currently serve	Ministries I would like to serve in	Thoughts and comments

Prayerfully consider where your talents would be best used for God's glory.

Whatever is true, whatever is noble, whatever is right, whatever is pure, whatever is lovely, whatever is admirable – if anything is excellent or praiseworthy – think about such things.
~ Philippians 4:8

What thoughts do you have that you shouldn't? What do you wish you thought about more? Ask God for help.

_____

_____

_____

_____

_____

_____

_____

_____

_____

_____

_____

_____

_____

I praise you because I am fearfully and wonderfully made; your works are wonderful, I know that full well. ~ Psalm 139:14

What are some things you like about the way God made you? Thank Him!

When I hear this song I feel close to God:

My feelings:

_____

_____

_____

_____

_____

_____

_____

_____

_____

_____

_____

_____

_____

Brothers, if someone is caught in a sin, you who are spiritual should restore him gently. But watch yourself or you also may be tempted.
~ Galatians 5:12

Who is someone you know is struggling with sin? Pray for them and consider how else you can help.

_____

_____

_____

_____

_____

_____

What is a sin you struggle with? Pray for help and think about a friend who might help you.

_____

_____

_____

_____

_____

_____

Be joyful always; pray continually; give thanks in all circumstances, for this is God's will for you in Christ Jesus. ~ 1 Thessalonians 5:16-18

How can you apply this verse to your life?

_____

_____

_____

_____

_____

_____

_____

_____

_____

_____

_____

_____

_____

_____

_____

_____

Use this page to pray for a prayer partner, special friend, or anyone in need of prayer. Put the person's name in the middle circle with prayers on their behalf on the lines.

Draw a picture of what you think the Garden of Eden looked like.

Sermon Notes - has your pastor ever preached something that made you feel like he was speaking directly to you?

Write about it here:

_____

_____

_____

_____

_____

_____

_____

_____

_____

_____

_____

_____

_____

_____

_____

_____

One of my favorite Bible verses:

Why it is special to me:

Bible Reading Goals:

My Goal: _____
This can be number of pages, chapters, or the whole Bible.
Make it work for you!

Let's Break it Down . . .

How many days?   _____

How many pages?   _____

Divide # of pages by # of
days to calculate how much
you need to read each day. _____

Now let's keep track of how you're doing.

Date	Page #

I urge, then, first of all, that petitions, prayers, intercession and thanksgiving be made for all people for kings and all those in authority, that we may live peaceful and quiet lives in all godliness and holiness. ~ 1 Timothy 2:1-3

Record below some leaders in your life (president, governor, mayor, boss, teachers, parents) and pray for them to seek God's will and lead according to it.

_____

_____

_____

_____

_____

_____

_____

_____

_____

_____

_____

_____

_____

Names of God

There are many names for God in the Bible, each revealing a different aspect of Him

Name of God	Meaning	Your thoughts
ELOHIM	God of power & might	
JEHOVAH-MACCADDESHEM	The Lord who sanctifies	
JEHOVAH-ROHI	The Lord my shepherd	
JEHOVAH-RAPHA	The Lord our healer	
JEHOVAH-JIREH	The Lord will provide	
JEHOVAH-SHALOM	The Lord is peace	
EL-OLAM	Everlasting Lord	
JEHOVAH-TSIDKENU	The Lord our righteousness	
JEHOVAH--YAHWEH	Our divine salvation	
EL-ELYON	Most high God	
JEHOVAH-SABBAOTH	Lord of Hosts	
EL-ROI	Strong one who sees	
EL-SHADDAI	God Almighty	

Advent

Therefore the Lord himself will give you a sign: The virgin will be with child and will give birth to a son, and will call him Immanuel. ~ Isaiah 7:14

Advent is the time that we celebrate the first coming of Jesus and look forward to His coming again. What are your thoughts on Advent?

_____

_____

_____

_____

_____

_____

_____

_____

_____

_____

_____

_____

_____

An angel of the Lord appeared to them, and the glory of the Lord shone around them and they were terrified. But the angel said to them, "Do not be afraid. I bring you good news of great joy that will be for all the people. Today in the town of David a Savior has been born to you; he is Christ the Lord."
~ Luke 2:9-11

What does our Lord's first coming mean to you?

_____

_____

_____

_____

_____

_____

_____

_____

_____

_____

Epiphany

After Jesus was born in Bethlehem in Judea, during the time of King Herod, Magi from the east came to Jerusalem and asked, "Where is the one who has been born king of the Jews: We saw his star in the east and have come to worship him."
~ Matthew 2:1-2

The 12th day of Christmas, or Epiphany, is the day that the manifestation of God in the human Jesus is celebrated. How do you celebrate it?

_____

_____

_____

_____

_____

_____

_____

_____

_____

_____

Ash Wednesday

For dust you are and to dust you will return.
~ Genesis 3:19

A day of repentance. Put your confession here.

_____

_____

_____

_____

_____

_____

_____

_____

_____

_____

_____

_____

_____

_____

_____

_____

After fasting forty days and forty nights, he was hungry. ~ Matthew 4:2

How do you remember and honor the sacrifice of Jesus during Lent?

_____

_____

_____

_____

_____

_____

_____

_____

_____

_____

_____

_____

_____

_____

Palm Sunday

Blessed is the king who comes in the name of the Lord! Peace in heaven and glory in the highest!
~ Luke 19:38

At the beginning of Holy Week, Jesus entered Jerusalem triumphantly as a king. How do you welcome him as your king?

_____

_____

_____

_____

_____

_____

_____

_____

_____

_____

_____

_____

Maundy Thursday

Jesus answered, "I am the way and the truth and the life. No one comes to the Father except through me." ~ John 14:6

Knowing Jesus is the only way to eternal life, how do you share salvation with others?

_____

_____

_____

_____

_____

_____

_____

_____

_____

_____

_____

_____

_____

Good Friday

With a loud cry, Jesus breathed his last. The curtain of the temple was torn in two from top to bottom. And when the centurion, who stood there in front of Jesus, heard his cry and saw how he died, he said, "Surely this man was the Son of God!"
~ Mark 15:37-39

Jesus died for you. How does that make you feel?

_____

_____

_____

_____

_____

_____

_____

_____

_____

_____

_____

You are looking for Jesus the Nazarene, who was crucified. He has risen! He is not here. ~ Mark 16:6

He lives! Jesus rose from the dead and will raise us to eternal life! Give Him thanks!

_____

_____

_____

_____

_____

_____

_____

_____

_____

_____

_____

_____

_____

_____

Pentecost

When the day of Pentecost came, they were all together in one place. Suddenly a sound like the blowing of a violent wind came from heaven and filled the whole house where they were sitting. They saw what seemed to be tongues of fire that separated and came to rest on each of them. All of them were filled with the Holy Spirit. ~ Acts 2:1-4

Have you asked the Holy Spirit to live in you?

_____

_____

_____

_____

_____

_____

_____

_____

_____

_____

_____

All Saints Day

Therefore, since we are surrounded by such a great cloud of witnesses, let us throw off everything that hinders and the sin that so easily entangles, and let us run with perseverance the race marked out for us.
~ Hebrews 12:1

The saints, those who have gone to heaven ahead of us, are the great cloud of witnesses surrounding, supporting, and praying for us. How does knowing this encourage you?

_____

_____

_____

_____

_____

_____

_____

_____

_____

_____

The King will reply, "Truly I tell you, whatever you did for one of the least of these brothers and sisters of mine, you did for me." ~ Matthew 25:40

Take a minute to think about someone who you have a difficult time loving. Pray for them and for yourself that your attitude can be like that of Jesus.

_____

_____

_____

_____

_____

_____

_____

_____

_____

_____

_____

_____

_____

_____

People who I can't wait to see in Heaven

Maybe they are people you know who have already had their Heaven Homecoming. Maybe you want to meet Biblical patriarchs who you've learned so much about. Write about them and what you think it might be like.

_____

_____

_____

_____

_____

_____

_____

_____

_____

_____

_____

_____

_____

_____

_____

_____

_____

"For I know the plans I have for you," declares the LORD, "plans to prosper you and not to harm you, plans to give you hope and a future."
~ Jeremiah 29:11

What does God want you to do? Pray for guidance.

_____

_____

_____

_____

_____

_____

_____

_____

_____

_____

_____

_____

_____

_____

_____

When I hear this song I feel close to God:

My feelings:

But grow in the grace and knowledge of our Lord and Savior Jesus Christ. To him be glory both now and forever! Amen. ~ 2 Peter 3:18

How do you grow in the grace and knowledge of our Lord?

_____

_____

_____

_____

_____

_____

_____

_____

_____

_____

_____

_____

_____

_____

And as for you, brothers, never tire of doing what is right. ~ 2 Thessalonians 3:13

When do you not like to do what you know is right? Ask God for help.

_____

_____

_____

_____

_____

_____

_____

_____

_____

_____

_____

_____

_____

_____

_____

_____

I am not ashamed of the gospel, because it is the power of God for the salvation of everyone who believes: first for the Jew, then for the Gentile.
~ Romans 1:16

Write about a time you were not ashamed to share the gospel. What about a time you wish you had?

_____

_____

_____

_____

_____

_____

_____

_____

_____

_____

_____

_____

_____

Though you have not seen him, you love him; and even though you do not see him now, you believe in him and are filled with an inexpressible and glorious joy. ~ 1 Peter 1:8

What do you think is the most visible evidence of Jesus?

_____

_____

_____

_____

_____

_____

_____

_____

_____

_____

_____

_____

_____

_____

_____

For you were once darkness, but now you are light in the Lord. Live as children of light (for the fruit of the light consists in all goodness, righteousness and truth) and find out what pleases the Lord. Have nothing to do with the fruitless deeds of darkness, but rather expose them. ~ Ephesians 5:8-11

How do you live as "children of light"? Have you ever had to expose "deeds of darkness"?

_____

_____

_____

_____

_____

_____

_____

_____

_____

_____

_____

_____

"Can anyone hide in secret places so that I cannot see him?" declares the Lord. "Do not I fill heaven and earth?" declares the Lord. ~ Jeremiah 23:24

Is there something you've been trying to hide from God? Confess it here.

_____

_____

_____

_____

_____

_____

_____

_____

_____

_____

_____

_____

_____

_____

You shall have no other gods before me.
~ Exodus 20:3

What "other gods" are you tempted to put before God?

_____

_____

_____

_____

_____

_____

_____

_____

_____

_____

_____

_____

_____

_____

_____

You shall not make for yourself an idol in the form of anything in heaven above or on the earth beneath or in the waters below. ~ Exodus 20:4

What are some common modern day idols?

_____

_____

_____

_____

_____

_____

_____

_____

_____

_____

_____

_____

_____

_____

_____

_____

You shall not misuse the name of the Lord your God. ~ Exodus 20:7

How do you show respect for the name of the Lord?

_____

_____

_____

_____

_____

_____

_____

_____

_____

_____

_____

_____

_____

_____

_____

_____

Remember the Sabbath day by keeping it holy.
~ Exodus 20:8

How do you recognize the Sabbath day and keep it holy?

_____

_____

_____

_____

_____

_____

_____

_____

_____

_____

_____

_____

_____

_____

_____

_____

_____

Honor your father and your mother, so that you may live long in the land the Lord your God is giving you. ~ Exodus 20:12

How do you honor your father and mother?

_____

_____

_____

_____

_____

_____

_____

_____

_____

_____

_____

_____

_____

_____

You shall not murder. ~ Exodus 20:13

Do you ever struggle with feelings of hatred? Confess and ask for help here.

_____

_____

_____

_____

_____

_____

_____

_____

_____

_____

_____

_____

_____

_____

_____

_____

_____

_____

_____

You shall not commit adultery. ~ Exodus 20:14

This clear command is often ignored and even mocked by our society. How do you keep it?

_____

_____

_____

_____

_____

_____

_____

_____

_____

_____

_____

_____

_____

_____

_____

_____

_____

You shall not steal. ~ Exodus 20:15

When is this command difficult to keep?

_____

_____

_____

_____

_____

_____

_____

_____

_____

_____

_____

_____

_____

_____

_____

_____

_____

_____

You shall not give false testimony against your neighbor. ~Exodus 20:16

Gossip is rampant and difficult to avoid. How do you deal with this widely accepted sin?

_____

_____

_____

_____

_____

_____

_____

_____

_____

_____

_____

_____

_____

_____

_____

_____

You shall not covet your neighbor's house . . . or anything that belongs to your neighbor.
~ Exodus 20:17

When are you tempted to feel jealous? How do you deal with jealousy?

_____

_____

_____

_____

_____

_____

_____

_____

_____

_____

_____

_____

_____

_____

_____

Going a little farther, he fell with his face to the ground and prayed, "My Father, if it possible, may this cup be taken from me. Yet not as I will but as you will." ~ Matthew 26:39

Write about a time when you did what you felt was God's will rather than your own or a time you wish you had.

_____

_____

_____

_____

_____

_____

_____

_____

_____

_____

_____

_____

_____

_____

And surely I am with you always, to the very end of the age. ~Matthew 28:20

What comfort do you receive from this verse?

\
\
\
\
\
\
\
\
\
\
\
\
\
\
\
\
\

Therefore go and make disciples of all nations, baptizing them in the name of the Father and of the Son and of the Holy Spirit, ~ Matthew 28:19

This command is known as The Great Commission. How do you help carry it out?

_____

_____

_____

_____

_____

_____

_____

_____

_____

_____

_____

_____

_____

_____

The angel said to the women, "Do not be afraid, for I know that you are looking for Jesus, who was crucified. He is not here; he has risen, just as he said." ~ Matthew 28:5-6

What does this verse mean to you?

_____

_____

_____

_____

_____

_____

_____

_____

_____

_____

_____

_____

_____

_____

_____

One of my favorite Bible verses:

Why it is special to me:

_____

_____

_____

_____

_____

_____

_____

_____

_____

_____

_____

When I hear this song I feel close to God:

My feelings:

The place where I feel closest to God is:

My feelings:

_____

_____

_____

_____

_____

_____

_____

_____

_____

_____

_____

_____

_____

_____

_____

_____

Favorite Quotes

How I spend my day

This circle is 24 hours. How do you spend them?

Pray for God to guide you in making good decisions regarding where you spend your time. What has changed since you last completed this exercise? Look back at page 70.

The best book ever:

Why I love it:

_____

_____

_____

_____

_____

_____

_____

_____

_____

_____

_____

_____

_____

_____

I praise you because I am fearfully and wonderfully made; your works are wonderful, I know that full well. ~ Psalm 139:14

What are some things you like about the way God made you? Thank Him!

While they were eating, Jesus took bread, gave thanks and broke it, and gave it to his disciples, saying, "Take it; this is my body." Then he took the cup, gave thanks and offered it to them, and they all drank from it. "This is my blood of the covenant, which is poured out for many."
~ Mark 14:22-24

What strength do you receive through Holy Communion?

_____

_____

_____

_____

_____

_____

_____

_____

_____

_____

_____

_____

_____

Consider it pure joy, my brothers and sisters, whenever you face trials of many kinds, because you know that the testing of your faith produces perseverance. Let perseverance finish its work so that you may be mature and complete, not lacking anything. If any of you lacks wisdom, you should ask God, who gives generously to all without finding fault, and it will be given to you.
~ James 1:2-5

How can these verses help you in difficult times?

_____

_____

_____

_____

_____

_____

_____

_____

_____

_____

My dear brothers and sisters, take note of this: Everyone should be quick to listen, slow to speak and slow to become angry, because human anger does not produce the righteousness that God desires. ~ James 1:19-20

How do these verses help put your anger in perspective?

_____

_____

_____

_____

_____

_____

_____

_____

_____

_____

_____

_____

_____

Use this page to pray for a prayer partner, special friend, or anyone in need of prayer. Put the person's name in the middle circle with prayers on their behalf on the lines.

I thank my God every time I remember you.
~ Philippians 1:3

Who are some people you are thankful God created?

Where are you now . . .

Look back at the beginning of this journal to the day that you started it. Let's look at some ways you have changed and grown since then.

Date: _____

How I think my relationship with God has changed:

_____

_____

_____

Some important things going on in my life are:

_____

_____

_____

How I have benefited from using this journal:

_____

_____

_____

Best Friend: _____

Christian Mentor: _____

My Church: _____

Where I live: _____

My favorite place to be: _____

My favorite thing to do: _____

Some of these preferences and things in my life have
changed. I think that is because:

_____

_____

_____

_____

This is where I see myself going from here:

_____

_____

_____

_____

Draw near to God and He will draw near to you.
~ James 4:8

Looking for help with . . .

Made in the USA
Charleston, SC
22 October 2012